# Masturbation Psychic Details

I0157799

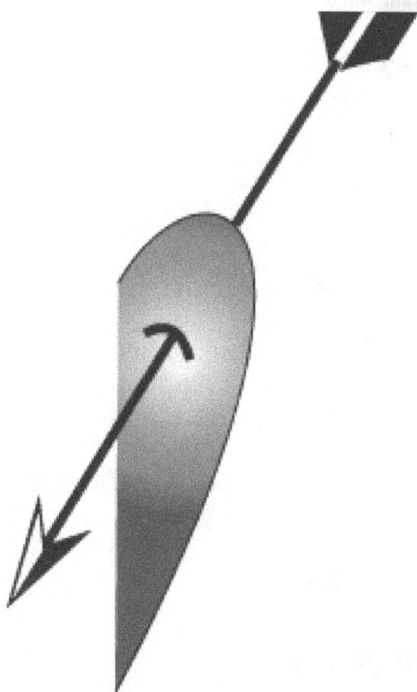

*Michael Beloved*

**Shiva Art:**     Sir Paul Castagna

**Illustrations:** author

**Proofreaders:** devaPriyā Yoginī / Marcia Beloved

**Questions of Interest** were generated by submissions of devaPriyā Yoginī, Alfredo Delregato and Dean Archer.

**Correspondence:**

Michael Beloved
18311 NW 8th Street
Pembroke Pines
FL  33029
USA

**Email:** axisnexus@gmail.com

**ISBN:** 978-0-9884011-3-6

**LCCN:** 2013909800

# Table of Contents

## *How to use this book:*

*Make a casual reading page for page without becoming stressed about the concepts and ideas. Read to become familiar with the language style and presentation. If you read something of particular interest make a mental note and read on to get through the entire book.*

*Make a second reading pausing at areas of interest, where you feel you can grasp the material. Here and there, you may not follow the meanings but read on nevertheless.*

*Make a third reading with intent to grasp the concepts and suggestions given.*

*Finally, make an indepth study of this information.*

# Introduction

*There is perhaps sufficient information about masturbation in the world today, both the pros and cons. Authors wrote extensively on the topic because it is interesting how a human being is driven for fulfillments of which sexual self-stimulation happens to be a prominent one.*

*This book presents the psychic side of the equation. Sex drive is primal in most sexually-mature human beings. It is very unforgiving if it is not fulfilled, where we find that we adopt anti-social activities and self-defeating behaviors when we do not cater it.*

*Evidence of this is the immoral behavior of many disgraced priests who, despite taking religious vows requiring sexual chastity, were unable to quell erotic desires. Some of this resulted in abusive perversions against children.*

*I jump into the discussion about masturbation on its psychic side. Really, there is sufficient literature in the world about the physical aspects, as well as with the emotional and mental forms of its fulfillments and frustrations.*

*There are doubts about the psychic side because it cannot be verified in an objective way except through subjective analysis which is something our primitive minds grapple with. Nevertheless you may read this information and cull from it some beneficial perspectives.*

**This answers queries of devaPriyā Yoginī,
one who has yogic interest
and who is dear (priyā) to God (deva).**

# Chapter 1

## Memory

Psychologically, masturbation is triggered by an urge or by the memory of a previous incidence. Memory, especially when it is very pleasurable or traumatic, influences the psyche to replay an incidence. The energy of a memory can instigate that a previous behavior be re-enacted physically.

*Where does memory originate?*

*Where, in the psyche, is it stored?*

*What is the subconscious?*

*How does memory motivate the physical body?*

**Location of Memory**

Please put aside the idea of the physical brain as the total means of memory. In this book, the memory is a psychic phenomenon, which affects physical actions. Memory is stored in the conscious and subconscious portions of the mind. New memories are located in the conscious mind; while old ones are stacked in chronological order in the subconscious.

Once a memory is formed in the conscious part of the mind, it remains there for a time. If it is not used regularly, it disappears into the subconscious chamber. As it transits to the subconscious it changes in form and becomes incoherent. For integral use by the conscious mind, memory has to be de-coded by re-exposure to the analytical intuition of the mind.

Memory energy has psychological weight, except that the heavier it is, the higher it floats. Very light-weight memories sink into the subconscious and have little buoyancy. The weight of a memory is caused by the interest value of it. If there is an event which is boring, then when the imprints are created, it will be light weight, which means that memory will slip into the subconscious where it would be supported by all previous subconscious imprints.

**Why does memory have weight? Why do the heaviest memories remain in the conscious mind while the light-weight memories quickly sink into the subconscious?**

Memory has weight because it is a subtle material energy. However in this case, the weight of a memory causes it to float upward, while materially we experience that weight causes objects to go downward. The weight of a particular memory is determined by its sensation-value in reference to the subject which the conscious mind considers. The more interest applied, the heavier the memory becomes.

The reach into the subconscious is done by the conscious mind upon request. The request might be sent by a sensual interest, a survival instinct, a desire or by the sense of identity. The intellect may make a request for a particular memory. When these requests are made a checking and converting energy goes into the subconscious and scans for related information. This is rescanned to be sure that it matches the criterion for the requested memory.

When a copy of this requested memory is acquired, the conversion into mental and emotional experience takes place. The copied memory is experienced in the conscious mind.

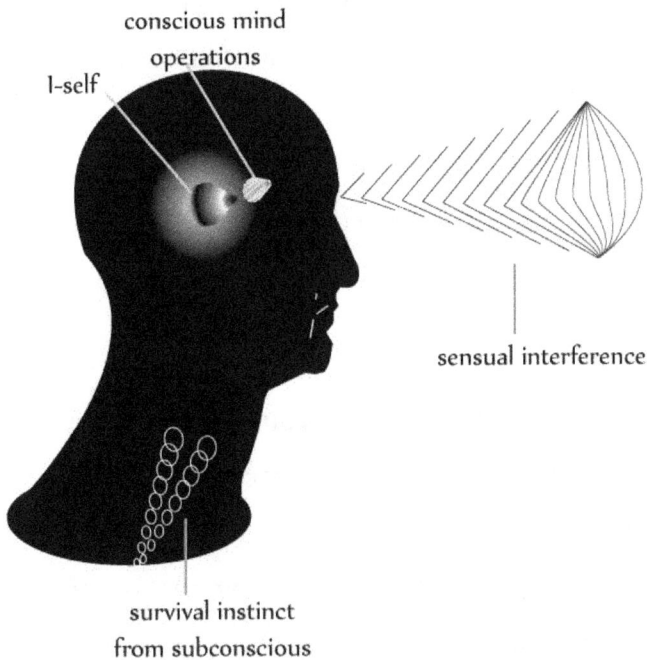

conscious mind
operations

I-self

sensual interference

survival instinct
from subconscious

After being handled by the conscious mind, the recently-displayed memory goes back into the subconscious with any new information which it acquired. This forms a new memory package in addition to the one which was in the memory before and which was copied.

In the incidence of masturbation, when it is done for the first time, a memory of it may remain in the conscious mind for a few days. Then this same memory recedes and enters the subconscious. Once it is in the subconscious it becomes unavailable except by request. The speed at which these requests are fulfilled is such that the person cannot realize that a copy of the memory moved from one part of the psyche to another.

Even after an incidence is converted into memory and moves into the subconscious, the memory leaves a super-subtle imprint of itself in the conscious mind. This is used by the observance portion of the mind. It reminds the psyche to again indulge itself at the nearest opportunity.

Before executing this command for a repeat performance, the analytical part of the mind will scan its records for any related incidences. If any are found, they are displayed in the mind. The scanning action of the analytical part may re-enforce or nullify the memory. If it reinforces, the desire will be manifested and the individual concerned will not have the power to stop the mind from commanding the body to masturbate.

If on the other hand it is nullified, then the individual may decide not to proceed. The idea will be forgotten with the memory of it sinking into the subconscious. It will form into an inhibition at a later date.

If however the nullified memory is disregarded by the individual, then another memory track will form in the conscious mind. This will release the inhibitive memory into the subconscious and further constrict the new memory track in the conscious mind. The individual will then be compelled to procure supportive energies which the psychic sensual mechanism will collect from the environment and contribute for the emergence of a strong urge.

This urge will compel the individual to act to complete masturbation.

Even though a first masturbation has no recent conscious or subconscious memory to support it, still that does not mean that there is no masturbation memory in the person's consciousness. There might be a memory deep within the ultra-subconscious. These ultra-memories are event deposits from previous lives as well as impressions which the person picked up before and during the fetal stage.

The ultra-memories required special interest for translation into conscious coherent information. Even if it is not translated, it may still enter into the conscious mind, mix with a current memory and cause a supportive or blocking influence.

A deep subconscious memory is not acquired by a request of the conscious mind. The deep-seated records from past lives, moved into the conscious mind independently on the basis of detection of a related current incidence. A deep memory discharges a copy of itself into the conscious mind. Then the individual concerned is forced to support it, even though he or she may have no idea of the components which motivated the special action commands.

## Storage of Memory

There are basically three memory storage compartments. These are psychological places, which cannot be discovered except through deep introspection or transcendental meditation. These are:

- Conscious mind memory in the head of the psyche
- Subconscious memory in the neck of the psyche
- Ultra-subconscious memory in the chest area of the psyche

I-self

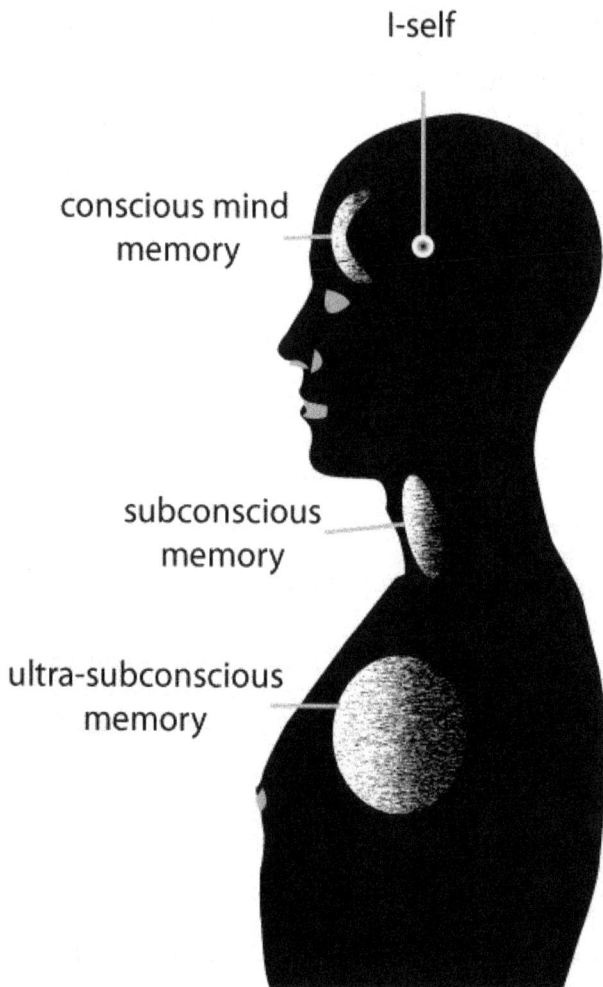

conscious mind
memory

subconscious
memory

ultra-subconscious
memory

The conscious mind memory is located in the frontal part of the head of the psyche. It holds recent memories and traumatic old memories which are habitually recalled by the individual. These memories are capable of the most rapid illustrations in the mind, and are predominantly from the current life.

The subconscious memory is located in the neck. This is memory from the present life span which was released from the conscious mind memory and is stored in the subconscious compartment in the lower part of the neck of the subtle body.

The ultra-subconscious memory is located in the lower part of the chest. These memories are from prenatal existences and are in a cryptic form which is not easily translated into coherent information. Despite its lack of coherence a pre-natal memory may have a bewildering influence on the person.

Coherent memories in the head of the subtle body are those which are recent and those which were recalled by the system from this or from a past life and which have relevance to a recent imprint.

The storage capacity of the conscious mind memory is limited. Any memory which is not used regularly is released from the bottom of the subtle head to pass into the neck and be deposited in the subconscious stock of memories.

There is a two-way feedback between the conscious and subconscious minds. There is a one-way feedback between the ultra-subconscious and conscious minds. There is no feedback between the subconscious and the ultra-conscious minds.

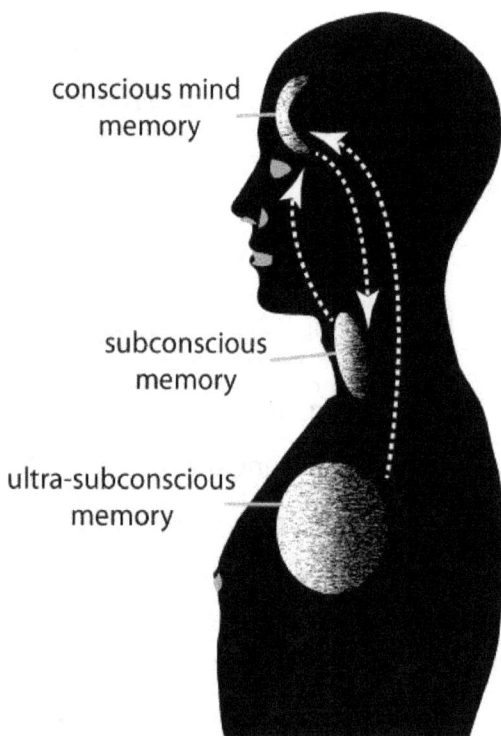

conscious mind memory

subconscious memory

ultra-subconscious memory

After death however, in the hereafter, and just when the entity fuses into the psyche of its would-be parents, the subconscious package of information about the entire recent lifetime becomes the top layer in the ultra-subconscious mind. It takes a one-way downward transport then but not during the physical life when that history was created.

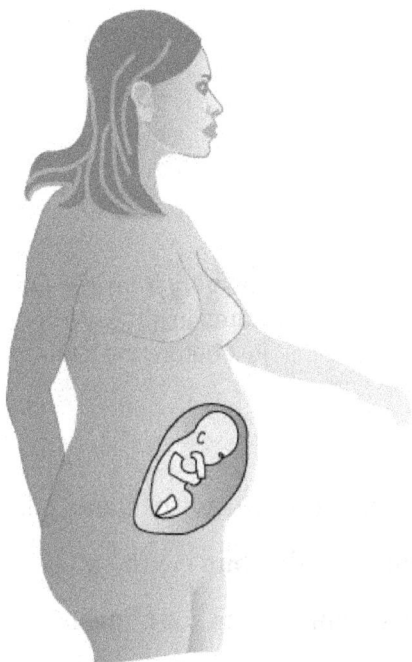

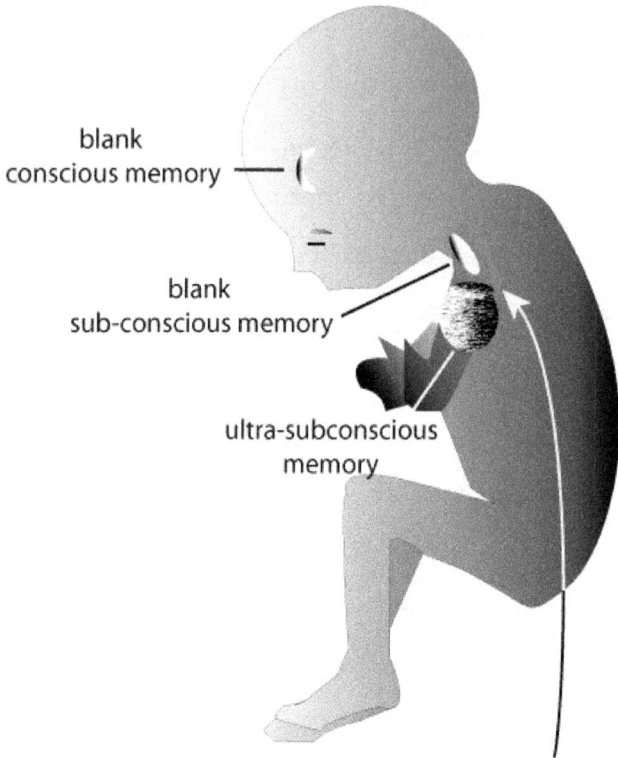

blank
conscious memory

blank
sub-conscious memory

ultra-subconscious
memory

top layer memory from immediate past life,
located in ultra-suconscious
just before the fetal stage.

We begin each new life with blank conscious and subconscious minds but with a content ultra-subconscious which has our past lives' history compacted into it, in an information format, which cannot be accessed.

| Past Life | Current Life | Potential Future Life |
| --- | --- | --- |
| flash memory of that past life | flash memory of this life | flash memory of the new life |
| subconscious memory accumulated in that specific life | subconscious memory of this life | subconscious memory created in the new life. |
| ultra-subconscious memory of previous lives, with no impressions from that specific life | ultra-subconscious memory of previous lives | ultra-subconscious memory of previous lives, including the subconscious memory created in the immediate past life |

Conscious to subconscious is a two way operation but conscious to ultra-subconscious is a one way operation always moving from ultra-subconscious to conscious. An advanced yogi or mystic may shift the observing self into the ultra-subconscious but coherent use of this cryptic information is limited by his insight capabilities. When information shifts from the ultra-subconscious to the conscious mind, it shifts with a conversion code which causes the information to convert into a disposition or attitude-approach in the conscious mind. When a yogi or mystic goes into the ultra-subconscious no such conversion apparatus becomes manifest. This means that reading information in the ultra-subconscious requires special transcendental intuition which is not available except in very deep meditation.

# Chapter 2

## Memory Formation

Whatever is witnessed, by any sense of the body, becomes a memory imprint in the psyche. Some of these have distinction, while some are so irrelevant as to have a faint imprint only.

Once a circumstance is witnessed either deliberately or non-deliberately, it causes the formation of an imprint in the head of the subtle body. This is memory from this life, which was recent or which was recently reviewed. If this memory loses prominence, it sinks to the bottom of the chamber. If it remains at the bottom and is not recalled, then it sinks through the neck and enters the subconscious.

The passage of this imprint from the conscious mind to the subconscious mind causes it to be compressed or flattened for storage. This is like when human beings desire to store a foodstuff. They may dehydrate it but in so doing its texture and mass are irretrievably altered.

## What is the subconscious?

The subconscious is a psychic chamber which holds mental and emotional impressions which were experienced by the conscious mind, and which fade from objective consciousness over time. The fading action is not the destruction of the memory. It is the accumulation of the memory in the subconscious chamber. When a memory is lost to the conscious mind, the same registers in the subconscious, but in a format which has to be converted before it can be used by the objective consciousness.

Memory which enters the subconscious does so in layers, one over the other according to the progression of time. This is an ordered system which is regulated by time factor in the particular realms where the events occur. Some of these layers have links with previous layers, such that if a memory is requested, its passage out of the subconscious causes other linked layers to be highlighted in the subconscious such that if the other related memories are required by the analytical mind, these layers will move instantly into the purview of the conscious mind.

While the conscious observing mind is in the frontal part of the head of the subtle body, the subconscious mind is located in the neck of the subtle body. Information which is conscious memory is psychological imprints which are in the head of the subtle body. Information which was transferred into the subconscious is not as readily available. There is psychic distance between the frontal part of the subtle head and neck region of the form.

## How does memory motivate the physical body?

Memory by itself is powerless to motivate a physical body. Conscious memory is more accessible than subconscious memory. However, both are powerless to act unless their effects influence the analytical or emotional energy of the psyche. In a sense, memory is quarantined emotional energy but as such it is energy with stored potential. For it to influence the unrestricted emotional energy in the psyche, it is handled by the analytic function of the mind.

This does not mean that memory has to be analyzed before it can influence what the mind will instruct the physical body to do. A memory may contact the analytical part of the mind or the emotional alert-energy which prevails at the time, and just by that contact without any other factor, the memory can cause the subtle body to move. That in turn will cause the physical system to operate because it is wired psychosomatically to mimic actions of the subtle form.

The physical system is like a shadow of the subtle body. Just as a shadow is seen to imitate the object which produces it, so the physical body imitates the actions of the subtle form. This may be accepted on the basis of thinking and then acting to manifest ideas.

Memories can be activated without special provocation or without sensual inputs where the mind feels that it has an associative impression. A memory can pop up or become visible in the mind without the individual doing or thinking anything which is related to it.

As fallen leaves blow in the wind, so subconscious memories, may on occasion, be affected by impulsive or random moods. As leaves on a tree shiver in the wind, so conscious memories may on occasion burst out without the person's request for them.

The most common effects of memory are felt when there is some input into the mind through the senses. Then that imprint is considered in the analytical portion of the mind which in turn sends a request to the subconscious for associative memories. If there are no related memories in the subconscious, the conscious mind will immediately send an imprint into the subconscious for storage. It does this by an automatic response mechanism which is run by the life force mechanism in the trunk of the subtle body.

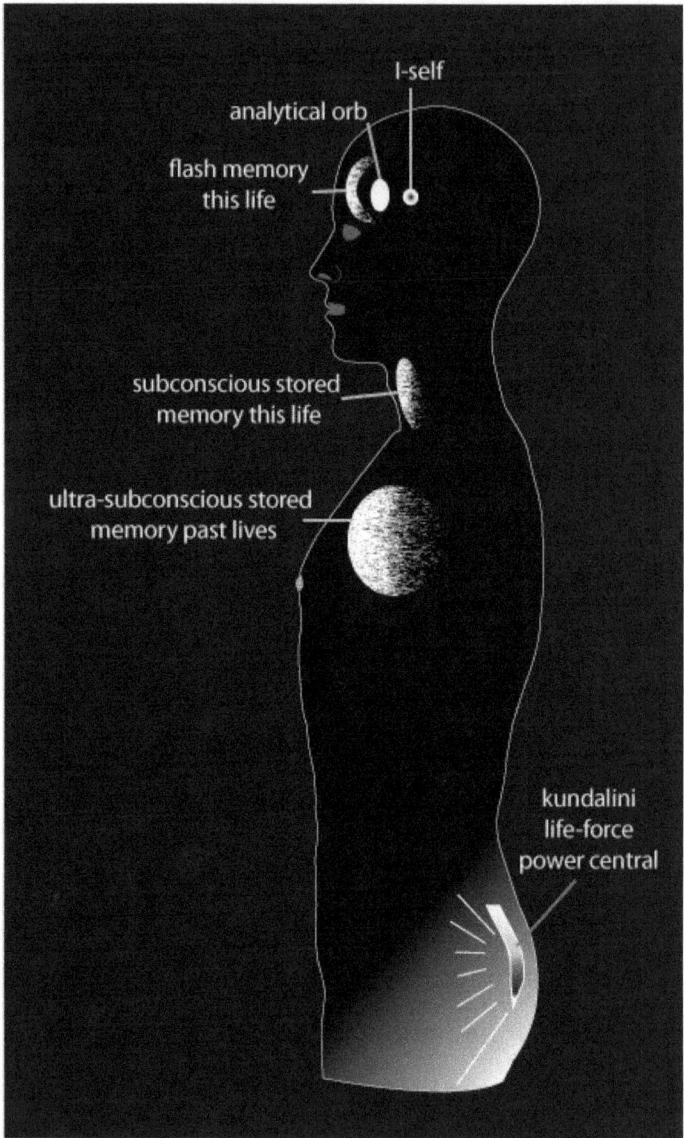

I-self

analytical orb

flash memory
this life

subconscious stored
memory this life

ultra-subconscious stored
memory past lives

kundalini
life-force
power central

This life force, when it senses that information is new and does not have an accessible memory, gives a command for the analytic part of the mind to store that information as a new unrelated imprint.

In the struggle for survival, the life force is keen to make notations about new impressions, since these may endanger the life of the physical body if they are not monitored. New impressions also bring in valuable information about new sources for exploitation. That is of keen interest to the life force which animates the body.

Apart from the sensual prompts for associative memories, the memories remain in the subconscious mind with a small psychic charge which is sufficient to cause a particular memory to be released if something is sensed which may be related to that stored impression.

These are memories which are released from the subconscious mind into the conscious mind without any request for their display. When this happens the self becomes influenced to pursue the memory and to make an effort to use it in the given situation. Even so this type of spontaneous release memory cannot motivate the self directly. It must influence the analytical part of the mind to give it consideration. If it is successful then its display to the core-self may cause actions which motivate the physical body.

Memory as an inactivated psychological tidbit of information cannot motivate a material body directly, but when it is linked into the analytical process, or when it is dissolved by emotional waves, its influence forms part of the impetus for physical movement.

The involvement between memory tit-bits and new incoming sensual data takes place automatically without any input from the entity concerned. This process though natural can be intercepted by the entity, if he (she) is trained to intercept transit emotions. Otherwise the individual is subjected to the ravages of the process of mental mixing for an advantage or a disadvantage caused by the analytical calculations.

# Chapter 3

## Memory Support System

The immediate source of a masturbation urge is the need for sexual release. In that there is the anticipation of a climatic experience. One remembers this climax on the basis of past experiences which are stored in the conscious and subconscious minds. Since these mental chambers are in the same psyche, they may be regarded as being different phases of the same energy or as being different parts of the psyche, which operate for self-preservation.

In my psychic research within the confines of my psyche, I found that the conscious and subconscious minds are distinct and separate. In fact the communication between these is a request-flow of energy from the conscious mind to the subconscious one, where the conscious mind accepts related information which is buried in the subconscious and which the conscious mind does not have in its possession.

Information stored in the conscious mind which is not used regularly or which the self does not like or avoids, will fall into the subconscious mind when it is released from the bottom of the conscious mind. It remains in the subconscious at the top of the heap of antiquated compressed information until another memory instance falls upon it.

When the conscious mind sends a request-energy to the subconscious, when supportive information is required, this request energy has the polarity and substance quality of the incidence in the conscious mind. It grips whatever it finds in the subconscious which has a similar resonance. It collects copy vibrations of old memories and takes these up into the conscious mind for review.

This does not happen with each and every idea which is in the conscious mind. This happens when the conscious mind needs reinforcement, justification    or    a    supportive    base    for    its considerations.

In the masturbation experience, if the individual concerned does not have sufficient confidence to complete the act, but wants to do it anyway, then the conscious mind sensing that uncertainty, will send down a request for any information which tallies with or which is similar to the masturbation activity which the psyche feels it needs to complete.

If there is no memory in the subconscious which tallies with the desire in the conscious mind, then the request energy will return into the conscious mind with a blank charge which will cause the conscious mind to be doubtful and disappointed. It will then check its information to see if it has sufficient impetus to carry out the urge. If it does not it may abandon the attempt or it may seek supportive influences which are given by sensual input from the environment outside the psyche.

# Chapter 4

## Urge

Urges are precursors of thought usually. Even when a thought about sexual expression is seen to produce or to activate an urge for it, still then we should assume that the urge was there before the thought.

The urge may support itself all on its own, where it does not need a thought process for boosting it. It may commandeer the entire body even if it does not get help from any other part of the psyche.

*What are the component parts of the urge?*

*Besides the masturbator, is there any entity, who is involved in the urge?*

*What is the psychic content of the urge?*

*What type of energy comprises the urge?*

**Remembering Masturbation**

Masturbation which is reinforced by memory of previous incidences is so definitely supported, that it may become a habit, which if the individual decides to abandon it, he or she will not be able to do so without a protracted struggle against it.

The memory of it is itself a danger to those who would like to abandon the habit. All the same, the memory is supportive to those who wish to continue the habit. In either case memory has importance but for those who want to quit, suppression of memory increases the person's resistance to the habit.

If someone wants to stop masturbation, that person should make every effort to stop the conscious mind from requesting supportive memories in the subconscious. In the mind the request for information from the subconscious is accompanied by a hope-projection energy, which anticipates that if the supportive memories are found, the person will have a grand orgasm and will be satisfied. It does not report on physical exhaustion and mental depression which might follow. When at last the exhaustion does manifest, the conscious mind is desensitized by the urge master in the body which is the kundalini life force. Then the observing I-self does not get the opportunity to deliberate sensibly on the issue. Thus the habit continues.

To scuttle the habit, the masturbator has to stop the discourse between the conscious and subconscious minds in this regard. The conscious self may make request for information from the subconscious which is supportive of quitting the behavior. This will produce a discouragement energy which will partially neutralize the urge.

Many statements in this book are so outlandish, as to border on the impossible and the ridiculous. I ask readers to trust in my knowledge of the psychic side of the existential border. On that side there are ancestors which are in the sexual energy of the masturbator. He or she is driven to act when one of these person-energies, becomes compressed and manifests in the psyche as a love expression source.

The pent up energies relate to the need for a material body, for an embryo.

A disembodied astral entity does not know that his (her) desire for an embryo will be frustrated if the possessed descendant masturbates. In the hereafter one only experiences the self as the sex urge of the descendant and feels that one should be expressed as a sexual discharge.

Masturbation has a dual source. In addition it involves a natural system of urges which are operated mostly by the psychic life force survival mechanism (kundalini). Whatever is physical must have a pre-source which is psychic or psychological. There must be a precursor for physical existence.

# Chapter 5

## Urge Components

Nature manufactures solid substances by super pressure of gaseous elements. If a block of wood was put to intense heat in a sealed container, the wood would disintegrate into ash and gas. If the ash were isolated and put under a larger amount of heat, that too would convert into gas dust.

The initial energy for masturbation is a psychic pressure which converts into subtle emotions, which are then transmitted into the psyche of the individual concerned. It is not all about the individual. It has to do with ancestral pressure. In the physical body of the individual, there are the urges which remain dormant until they are triggered by psychic actions which cause them to be surcharged with a purpose which is to be ejected from or in the body of the individual.

The interpretation of the mind just before masturbation is usually the personal need of the individual concerned without recognition of other psychic pressures and energy injections which victimize the individual. Once a psychic pressure penetrates the individual's emotion, he or she may identify with the energy as his or hers, and has to comply with the urges or feel frustrated if pressures prevent the performance.

The urge is one factor but it has parts which make it a molecular psychic force. Within the urge there is the hormonal energy of the body, the conjoint psychic pressure for reproduction, the helplessness of the individual concerned and the organ's response to the urge. If these are unified, the individual is compelled to seek a place to perform the masturbation.

When the individual endures the discharge of fluids either in a pleasant, unpleasant or intensely pleasurable way, there is a feeling of relief. The organ may lose sensitivity. The urge energy may assume a vacant configuration and the work begins for the fluids discharged to secure reproductive development. Since masturbation is the stimulation of one organ and since reproduction requires a male and female involvement, the discharged fluid fails in its mission to develop an embryo.

The failure of the individual to realize the energy of others is due to the fact that the energy of the others fuses into the emotional content of the psyche. If water is discharged into water, differentiating the additional liquid is daunting task. When disembodied souls enter into the psyche of a human being, the person who is possessed can hardly sort his or her emotions from that of the others. It requires a very sensitive mind to know that one's energies are boosted by that of disembodied souls.

## How do the ancestors express an influence which causes a human being to masturbate?

The influence of the ancestors is a psychic pressure which surfaces in the mind of the human victim as a need for sexual energy release. The influence of the ancestors is so abstract that the human victim does not recognize it as an alien input. Due to physical focus, the human victim is insensitive to subtle motivation and mistakes promptings from others as his or her desire.

The flood of lusty energy which sponsors masturbation is considered by the individual to be his or her need, making the act of masturbation unquestionable and free from a source analysis. This is quite suitable for a discharge of sexual energy to reduce the stress caused by the influx of desire energy from the ancestors.

A person who passed away may become an impulse for lust only, and may not deliberately victimize anyone. Based on past life social conditions, that person is attracted to a human victim to whom there is some consequential connection on the basis of services performed by the deceased in the past life.

The departed soul does not have to be objectively aware of the relation in the past life. Psychic nature is polarized. Those who performed social services in a particular family or society, automatically take advantage of anyone who benefits from those past activities.

Once it becomes an urge for a new embryo, for being in social circumstances of physical existence, the departed soul may enter into the emotions of anyone to whom its previous social life has caused a substantial benefit. It is not protected from contraceptive methods necessarily but still its influence will prevail and may surface in a way that causes repeated masturbations.

The ancestor who is in the psychic energy of a human being cannot sort between masturbation and a heterosexual fertile possibility for an embryo. It is not situated with the necessary psychic objectivity to determine this. It only has subjective access to the lust energy of a sexual discharge. As such it may repeatedly enter into the sex energy of a human being and be repeatedly discharged without ever acquiring an embryo.

Once it becomes a sexual urge-energy in the victim's emotional body, it functions as a sexual urge only. It is not perceived as anything else either by itself or by the victim. The victim may masturbate repeatedly to express this urge but since there is no embryo created, the particular ancestor who is the urge will re-enter into the sexual organs again and again, continuously inspiring repeated self-stimulation.

The ancestor is not deliberately targeting the masturbator, and still the result of ancestral influence is a targeted urge which affects the human concerned.

## What rights have they?

The rights of the ancestors to inhabit the emotions of a human being, are based on previous social endeavors, made by specific ancestors in the family line of the victim. It is not that the ancestor seeks to assert that right necessarily. In fact irrespective of the attitude of the ancestor, the energies themselves latch on to descendants by a psychic attraction which is based on the social work done in past lives by the ancestral spirit involved.

In most cases there is no deliberate influence to urge masturbation. It happens as a matter of course as the social equations are solved out in the layout of providence. In some cases, the person who is in the urge energy is quite different to the person whom the masturbator might conceive of as a possible mate during the self-stimulation. It may be that the energy involved is a complexity, where three prominent factors and other lesser stimuli are involved.

These are:

- The physical actor
- The psychic contributor (deceased person)
- The mate who is physically absent (or present)

The deceased person(s) lives in the psyche of the physical actor as an urge.

In the fantasy of the physical actor, the psychic mate is involved on the mental and emotional levels to help with the process of expressing and then fulfilling the urge through orgasm.

The deceased person who functions as the urge is frustrated. The physical actors lose energy but gain the satisfaction of the orgasmic relief. A mate who is absent may or may not be conscious of the incidence.

The persons who gain the most from such an alliance are the physical actor and the mate. The fulfillment is the greatest on the psychic plane. There is encouragement for the act coming from the deceased contributor. Some physical actors imagine that a psychic being is present when in fact there are impressions of that psychic being which were absorbed sensually or through media exposure.

The ancestor, psychic contributor, who functions as the urge only, is to be pitied in this situation since that disembodied person does not experience himself or herself in a way which can command a heterosexual alliance which is the traditional method for acquiring an embryo.

The physical actor and absent mate may get some pleasure, some fulfillment of the urge but the ancestor who is the urge gets frustration only, and a very abstract sense of frustration at that, something which later will manifest as an unruly and very demanding childhood for whoever becomes the parent eventually.

# Chapter 6

## Psychic Nature

The question arises as to why life is not simpler, as to why there is a psychic component which most human beings cannot perceive.

The answer is that nature is complicated. It is complex with many intertwining levels which may on occasion give or prohibit insight. As products of life, we are tiny portions of the blend with some objectivity and with a massive subjective consciousness which does not impart to us the perspectives of the events.

Under the display of physical nature is psychic nature which is enduring in reference and which serves as the support for everything which becomes physically manifested. Our focus is on personality but in the designation as human beings or as pet animals and not as any other format of life. Thus psychic urges which are personality conversions are not recognized by us as anything but urges, as faceless energies without individual features.

This allows us to masturbate with no inhibitions and with sexual intrigues which are a disappointment and rabid frustration for the ancestors whose sole interest is to become an embryo. First the ancestor is an urge. If it gets into a fertile female body, it becomes an embryo, which evolves into being a child, which becomes a juvenile and then an adult human being. If there is no fertile situation then the entity remains as an urge and does not perceive itself as anything else.

*Was I a sexual urge when I was disembodied?*

*Did I victimize my parents as described?*

*If I am not this body, and only possess it since its initial formation as a sperm particle in the father's body, then how is it that I feel as if I am this body and the urges of it are mine?*

*Can I be freed from these urges?*

*What are my rights?*

*Would it be fair for me to disown the urge-energies?*

# Chapter 7

## Complexities of the Urge

Perhaps the majority of persons, who masturbate as a regular or rare feature of the lifestyle, feel that it is a desirable feature of life. A few persons however feel that it is undesirable and wish for its conclusion. Wishes are wishes. Some have insufficient impact to reverse what is undesirable.

The desirability may disable a person's interest in studying the psychic content of the act. Even so, some who likes to masturbate would be informed if they gained insight into the components of the action. If masturbation is a conjoint act between a physical being and a psychic one(s) then how is that unity forged?

*Is the physical agent bringing it on?*

*Is the agent merely being induced into this in a surreptitious manner where he or she assumes control as allowed by the subtle presence of the disembodied person?*

*What would happen if the physical agent saw the departed ancestor who is involved?*

**If someone is possessed by a disembodied spirit who will be discharged in sexual energy, then how is masturbation which results from that influence, any different to masturbation which has no disembodied spirit content?**

One should assume that sexual energy always has disembodied spirit content.

**Does it matter if I am possessed by a disembodied soul whose sexual energy merged into mine and influences my behavior?**

One should assume that one is always influenced by departed ancestors.

John met a girl to whom he became attracted. He spoke to her in the ice-cream shop and offered to pay for her selection. She declined. John thought for sure that he should get to know this person intimately but she rejected his entreaties.

Just before she left the shop she looked at him and smiled. John loved that smile. He cherished it in his mind again and again after she left and disappeared in the distance.

Later during the night, remembering her, John began to masturbate. As he did so he envisioned the girl. He felt a strong urge to pass sexual fluids into the girl's sexual passage.

*Was this the result of John's energy and mental imagery of the girl's form which his mind photomapped?*

*Was anyone else involved?*

*Was there a departed soul(s) mixed into those energies which entered into John's body in the hope of getting a body, through John's potential for intercourse with the girl?*

**Affection control**

*Is masturbation inclusive of affection energy or is it completely devoid of that?*

*If the masturbator had access to a sexual partner, would the expression of sexual energies include an affectionate response from either partner?*

If affection energy is part of an urge, the power in the urge may subside if the affection is squelched. If the person is disinclined from the urge for whatever reason, extracting the affection-content may disable the fantasy.

**Since affection is enjoyable, why not suppress or eliminate some other aspect?**

The problem with that suggestion is that affection is easily one most of the recognizable symptoms to identify. Before a person can eliminate a component of an urge, that component must be identified. Once it is identified the person concerned should test to see if the component can be handled. Many subtle aspects of life cannot be perceived directly, which means that they cannot be interfered with by the person.

**Love affairs are usually highlighted by petting, kissing, fondling and giving affections in the most desirable way. Are these components of a love act also present in masturbation?**

**Who would be the child?**

An act of masturbation in which the sexual fluids of the male made no contact with genitalia of a fertile female would not result in a pregnancy. But if there was contact and there developed a pregnancy, who would be the infant?

*Was this infant part of the urge for the intercourse which produced its embryo?*

*If this was removed from being a composite part of the urge, would the masturbation not occur due to lack of sufficient sex drive?*

Affection energy is a composite of any sex related expression. This is because affection is emotion. Emotion, in turn, has concentrated hormonal energy as its medium of transmission within the psyche of the self. Affection has made a good name for itself among human beings but it does sponsor distress and does convert into frustration regularly. In its undesirable converted forms it is not recognized as affection. Thus it stands its ground as being acceptable to humans.

In masturbation, the entity is subjected to flashes of insight about those to whom affections were directed previously. These mental interruptions serve as psychological supports for the act. During the performance bits of affection data radiate from the self. There are receptions of affection packages from others, which were being broadcast at the moment, or were broadcast earlier and then were stored in the psyche or floated in the air around the individual.

If the individual tracks the affectionate energies which roam in the psyche during the masturbation, there would be a discovery of the composite individuals involved. This does not mean active involvement. It may for instance be passive involvement or even subconscious participation. It may be a contribution of affection which is so abstract as to not be recognized by anyone.

**What should the masturbator do once there is discovery of the affections of others embedded in the urge? If you are not the only agent, then how should your liability be structured?**

One way to face this is to consider what would happen if the sexual energy expressed was shared with the fertile body of a partner of the opposite sex.

## Masturbation as self-sex

Masturbation may be regarded as a case of self-sex, as an individual being in love with itself. For this theory to hold up we should prove that there is no other person-components beside the one observing self in the psyche.

If departed spirits can enter the psyche of those who are living, then masturbation disqualifies as self-sex. If there are more than one you in you, then the percentage of your contribution to masturbation should be determined. You may have a small percentage of control, while other persons who are in the urge-energy, may exhibit much more influence and desire.

*What happens to your disposition when you realize that there are other influences, that others, departed spirits and/or physical beings, are part of the mix of the energy which is the urge?*

*Is the release of energy a dispossession where someone, a departed spirit say, is expelled from your body in the sexual energy released.*

*Would the person repossess your body and cause it to again develop the urge, and to again need the release. How often would this happen?*

## Multiple features in females

By anatomical design, the discharge of sexual fluids in a female cannot result in the pregnancy in a male body. Orgasms in the males and females result in the discharge of fluids but the male body has no uterine access. Therefore even though the females have a residual male instrument in the form of a clitoris, the males are not permitted the biological advantage of even a rudimentary vaginal passage with uterine facility for developing fetuses.

Females are uniquely gifted with uterine access and a rudimentary male facility which does provide a discharging bliss aspect. To sort it, we would have to accredit females with sexual discharge of the clitoris and also sexual discharge in the vaginal passage and uterine facility. This is a huge advantage over males with their one discharge facility.

Masturbation in females is complex as compared to that in males, with female having the edge in every respect. Medical science now uses masturbated fluids of both males and females but with special emphasis on male sperm. For females the value is in the retrieval of eggs while for males it is in sperm collection.

Even so, by virtue of anatomical construction, the females have the lead. Their bodies can use masturbated fluids from a male body to produce an embryo and it can also use eggs from another female in the production of an embryo.

*What can the males do in this regard?*

They are anatomically disadvantaged. They can neither cater to sperm even their own or ovum for the production of fetuses.

It seems that the varieties of sexual expression which females have, far outpace that of the males with their one way system of sexual energy accumulation and discharge. Without drugs and other aids, men are only capable of one, for the most two or three, sexual discharge experiences within twenty four hours with the accompanying pleasure experiences. For women it is quite different.

The complexity of the woman's sexual apparatus is itself the reason why they have the advantage to where their sexual pleasure capacity borders on the unlimited, not to an absolute degree but in comparison to the very restricted expression men are allowed. Still, we find that men carry a conceited self-conception which is not borne up by facts.

For many a hard shell there is a soft interior. Some soft exteriors have a tough inner. Such is the intrigue of nature.

Males have a natural one shot chance at ejaculation, after which unless drugs and some other means are used, they must wait until nature develops the next charge. It's not so with females.

# Chapter 8

## Questions of Interest

**Will masturbation bring unfavorable repercussions in a future life?**

Masturbation has consequences in the present life time. It could like any other human behavior have impact on a future life. In so far as it serves to disenfranchise ancestors, it is, technically speaking, a psychic crime. Any human behavior which results in blocking the birth of an ancestor who has right to take birth, because of that departed soul's previous social contributions, may bring unwanted circumstances in the future.

The consideration should be a selfish one, where the masturbator considers what would be his or hers reaction if the situations were switched. If I, the living human, was on the astral side with desperate hopes of being a living human being again, how would I feel if I was deprived of an embryo by a relative of mine whom I cared for in my former life? Even if I was not aware of reincarnation, still I would feel disenfranchised, turned away, spurned as it was, and would suffer from frustration, disappointment and depression.

*How would my negative attitude affect the masturbator?*

**If done in moderation, is masturbation physically or psychologically healthy or unhealthy? Is it good or bad for the cardiovascular system? Is it good or bad for one's wellbeing?**

A physical behavior which is healthy may not benefit the individual on the psychological or emotional level. An act which gives emotional relief may be beneficial for one individual and harmful to another. Serial killers get relief from their vicious acts but at the expense of the lives of others.

Masturbation should be considered in a wider swath involving the physical and psychological interaction of energy. If we could pin down the psychic or emotional cause of it, and if we could tend to that successfully then there would be a noticeable reduction in it.

Of course that is ideal. Still, if we could tend to the actual cause we would at least lessen the formation of the urge, resulting in a decrease in the incidences.

The buildup of sexual energy and the inability to release it shows that we are unable to transcend or even to change the way those biological and emotional energies operate.

**Why do some women reach orgasmic sexual pleasure quickly while others endeavor even for hours and are unable to reach climax? Does this imply something about fate or the consequences of a previous life (lives)?**

We are in a conjoint situation where many incidences occur without us being major contributors or causes. It is a vast universe. We exist now some billions of years since this began. It makes sense to see that we are not causes but are effects of causes and will continue as the effects of effects even hereafter. One part of this planet, the extreme North is cold, while on the equator it is perpetually warm. It just happens to be that way. No vegetation at the equator should feel that it is the cause of its fortunate existence. Vegetation in the tundra should not feel that it is the cause of its sad stunted state.

The sexual capacity, or the lack of it, has more to do with the genetic format of the body than anything else. It depends on the ancestral biology, the food one was fed as an infant, the chemicals in the environment and many other factors which are beyond control. Someone is lucky; some other person is unlucky; like the throw of dice in a game.

In this creation both persons and things are playthings of fate, irrespective of their good or bad, suitable or unsuitable forms.

It is all about experience, the good, the bad, the unfortunate incidences and the endearing ones. What is culled finally is experience. Of course we prefer pleasant and enjoyable circumstances but nature affords the contrary all the same.

**Do you consider it as God's gift to women that many women are capable of limitless orgasmic experiences to the point of stopping only because of exhaustion due to the fact we have to endure the emotional traumas of putting up with men as well as the pain of menstruation and child birth?**

This creation came about as it came about and was not planned the way a human city planner instructs an architect in a draft room.

*Why just women, what about the rest of the female species, at least the mammals?*

*Are all female mammals exploiting limitless sexual pleasure as compared to the males of their species?*

*Why single out the human species since their bodily desire is so similar as the other mammals?*

Men are part of the layout of material nature. They did not create themselves. They came about as nature evolved just as females did. Thus if anything we should accredit or discredit nature. The females did not create themselves either. Whatever they can enjoy or exploit which men cannot, is just what nature dictated to be the capacity of their experience.

**Do men feel cheated and resentful that women easily get the experience of multiple orgasms, instead of being restricted to one, two or three within twenty-four hours?**

Each species and each gender of each species have its advantages and disadvantages as ordained by the construction of the body used. Usually men are not aware of the sexual pleasure capacity which women enjoy. Each person is restricted to their own mental and emotional feeling and responses. This is why it is all about experiences. Assuming reincarnation, assuming that one takes various bodies in various species from time to time, one gains experiences of this or that life form and carries the impressions from that in one's psyche when one goes to another life either in the same species or into a different life form, or a different gender in the same or some other life form.

Irrespective of the advantage I have today, that may not be available in the next transmigration. I may be the Queen today and the servant of the Queen in the next life.

## What is your remark about the male chauvinistic tendency in respect to women?

Ultimately the fault in anything has to be placed on Nature itself, since nature must first create the item or the life form. This is not a system of making excuses for individual behavior but under the good or bad pattern there has to be some natural support or it could not occur. Any possibility which becomes a reality must be supported by nature or it could not exist.

In the case of errant behaviors, even though nature endorsed the activity, still there may be dire repercussion from nature and/or from the human or animal society in which the behavior is manifested. The endorsement of nature or its permission or encouragement for a behavior is not necessarily a protection from adverse reactions.

**Would it be correct to say that for the average human being, there is nothing in the world more powerful than a woman's sexuality?**

This is also a feature of nature, where it exhibits itself through women in an irresistible way. Life on earth for the human species is initiated through embryonic development in the body of a female. Nurturing of infant forms is done primarily on the basis of nutritional support from the body of a female. Nature designed the sociology in that way. This makes women the hub of reproduction. In production of embryos, the woman acquires the raw material in the form of sperm and produces the finished production in the form of a live birth.

**Is there any significance in some women's experience of orgasms during childbirth or breast feeding?**

The electrical circuit in the body which triggers nerve responses is wired in such a way that the psychic or physical touching of the female organ and breasts, could result in orgasm. Some persons, male and females, experience orgasms when viewing nude photos or videos. This means that their visual perception is in some way hard-wired to the sexual drive.

Sex is a natural function. Even without the self desiring involvement through sex, still by nature's command, a person has the sex drive which nature develops at puberty, maximizes in young adult life and gradually simmers down in the elderly years.

**Does masturbation have a spiritual origin?**

Masturbation is not a spiritual circumstance or compulsion. It is based on sex energy storage and release. This has to do with using a material body and not being able to regulate its storage of sex hormones. From a biological perspective, masturbation is the individual's lack of control of the endocrine system. The individual did not invent the system. He or she does not have and did not have full control of it at any stage.

## Why does masturbation happen?

The powerful attribute of the sex energy in the human body is a biologically-given aspect. Nature it seems has caused this energy to be impulsive because of nature's interest in propagating the species. Once a species of life is manifested physically anywhere, then nature has the task to continue that species. Since the bodies are short-lived, nature has this system of reproduction to create a transit from a dying body to one that can reproduce new forms.

## Is the orgasm a spiritual phenomenon which makes us aware of happiness in the spirit world?

Physical body sex orgasmic experience does have a bliss aspect to it, but it is not spirit based. The electric charge of it comes from material nature, based on the foods eaten by specific species. Genital focus for a bliss-aspect pleasure indicates an insufficiency in the overall bliss aspect of a particular form, where the stress for pleasure is genitalia-focused. Variety spiritual bliss (hladini – Sanskrit) renders evenly out of every part of a spiritual body with no special aspect in the genitals. In the spiritual environments, there is no application of the mundane sex drive as we experience it in the material world.

**If someone is habituated to masturbation can that behavior ruin a heterosexual marriage relationship? Could it be the cause for sexual frustrations and resentments?**

Once a person finds a method of masturbation which brings great pleasure; that might become the preferred method of sex energy release. Thus if that person acquires a partner of the opposite sex, and if that sexual intercourse does not yield an equivalent or greater intensity of sexual pleasure, there is the likelihood that the relationship might be undervalued. Depending on the cultural environment, this might lead to divorce.

**Some women say heterosexual sex does not give them the degree of pleasure they achieve by masturbation, where they can target the pleasure producing part of the genitalia more effectively than occurs during intercourse with man.  How does this figure in?**

Since some and not all women make this claim, the pleasure-location yielding design of the sexual organs must vary from person to person. Even so the psychic aspect of masturbation should be considered, as to other psychic entities who are in it.

*Is there any other person on the psychic side who is involved in it?*

*Does an unseen participant contribute anything to the burst of pleasure?*

*What will happen if those other contributors withdraw support?*

On occasion, a person who has a sexual arousal finds that it disappears with no idea of how it ceased.

*Could it be that some psychic actor became absent and that contributor's energy was withdrawn causing the collapse of the urge?*

## Some people claim that in reference to physical orgasm, dream sex release is much more intense. What is the reason for this conclusion?

Dream life is the use of the subtle body when it is partially or fully de-synchronized from the physical one. Without the physical body fused with it, the subtle body has increased psychic perception which would result in more intensity of any sensual experience. Some dream experiences may feed over into the physical system. Some may only be acted on the subtle plane without transfer to the physical level.

## Is masturbation more normal at certain ages, like for example, during adolescence?

Masturbation is as normal as the libido sex drive in human beings. It is a development in the process of expressing sexual energy. Animals like billy-goats, bulls and dogs were seen masturbating. It is not a frequent habit in most of the species but it is an outcome of the need for sexual expression.

Masturbation does vary according to bodily age but only with the same underlying need for its climatic fulfillment. Once it develops as a habit, the slightest trigger may cause the person to complete it. It can be a compulsive disorder.

## From the yogic viewpoint is masturbation a sexual perversion?

From the yogic viewpoint masturbation is an unwanted behavior. Ideally a yogi should either desist from sexual activity completely or should be engaged in it in a morally responsible way. An argument arises as to what is sexual morality.

In the yogic way of thinking, morality is defined by material nature in terms of how it process and then reconfigures the energies involved in an action. This may or may not tally with human views of moral behavior.

If one takes a dog's body, one will have to wag the tail to express happiness. If one takes a frog's body, one will croak loudly when the rainy season begins. It all depends on the body used. Some human bodies have a submerged sexually which is not easily aroused, making masturbation unnecessary but there are other human body types which have a dramatic sexual urge which makes sex restraint an impossibility.

A student yogi should study his body and its capacities. Then he can either reinforce its good tendencies or curtail them. Nature enforces practicality and is not parry to mere concepts of idealism. Study the tendencies of your body. Then plan to reform it from unwanted behaviors.

**Assuming that reincarnation is a fact, and that ancestors do possess semen, what is the liability for deliberately ejaculating semen outside a woman's sexual passage either in self stimulation or during intercourse with a partner.**

The result of not developing an embryo is frustration in the emotional body of the entity concerned, the particular ancestor. His or her unsuccessful repeated effort to acquire a body, by being a primary part of an urge for orgasm, causes frustration.

At a later date, that negative energy will target the person(s) who deprived the ancestor. This may manifest in the same life or in another life.

A fisherman knows that hooks and knives are dangerous and yet he uses these on a daily basis. On occasion the danger becomes evident in the form of a gash on his hand. Knowing that masturbation will disenfranchise an ancestor may not be sufficient to stop the behavior, just as the fisherman's knowledge about sharp tools, does not totally prevent him from being harmed.

Yogis are supposed to live in isolation, away from the haunts of human beings. Yogis have the authority to be anti-social and to avoid human association. Done successfully, this protects the yogi from making contact with sexually-inclined entities. There is a reality called fate. It has the sum total responsibility. It may pressure a yogi to copulate. Or it may cause sexual arousal which has to be concluded through masturbation. A yogi should do his best to side-step sexual association and he must also be compliant with fate.

The student yogi, however, does not have that protection in the subtle existence, except that there no progeny is produced. In the subtle world, one can have sex for sex's sake without the risk of a pregnancy.

**Is it true that masturbation is an opening to the dark astral/vital forces? Is it an insinuation from these forces that feed psychically/astrally on the energy generated by the masturbator, propitiating temporary possessions and perversions?**

Masturbation certainly involves ancestral energy and ancestral personality.

*How should I relate to this?*

*Do I owe my grandmother a favor on the basis of what she did for this body's development in the embryonic state and after its delivery?*

*Am I the only legitimate proprietor to any service this body might render?*

*Do I have an inalienable right to disenfranchise my ancestors from taking birth through this body?*

*Am I responsible for their upkeep if they take an embryo from my body?*

**It seems that it would be impossible to attain urdhva retas upward-flowing semen state if one masturbates.**

This would apply to student adepts who have not curbed kundalini shakti. Once kundalini is curbed, the recommendations for no sexual expression may on a rare occasion be ignored by the ascetic. And yet, this does not mean that the ascetic should become careless.   At any moment, the subtle body may resume an unwanted behavior. Then the yogi will find himself on a lower plane of consciousness with a lifestyle which that level supports which may not be accommodating to spiritual progress.

Generally speaking it is like a hydraulic system, where if there is a leak somewhere, the system cannot hold pressure and becomes dysfunctional. If the ascetic loses vital energy in a lower chakra it will not be possible to get that same energy to rise into the head.

If kundalini is attracted to the lower chakras and wants to derive its pleasures there, the higher chakras will be of no interest to it. Most of the energy will be expended on the lower levels.

**What is the relationship between subconscious urges (vasanas) and masturbation? The insinuation, whether foreign or inner, starts as an impetus that should be rejected each time, but if the urge for masturbation arises in the mind, it is almost as if the arrow has left the bow and cannot be retrieved. A manifested urge is said to arise always to commit suicide, meaning**

**to fulfill itself. Fantasies about sexual expression could lead to masturbation.**

Subconscious impressions can be dealt with if one goes into deep meditation. From the surface level of consciousness one cannot stop a subconscious influence which is manifested to the conscious mind. This is because its manifestation will not be obvious and will not have a means for the observing self to terminate it.

It is exactly like someone who is destined for suicide. If his desire is hidden from his family, they cannot stop him from completing it. Even in one's mind, there are energies, urges, and tendencies, which are hidden from the very self and which will play out their potency to achieve whatever they are destined to affect.

In very deep meditation one can confront these energies and determine whether they are empowered by fate or not. But from the ordinary level of consciousness this is not possible and one will have to submit to their process.

**Is it true that masturbation is a sexual perversion with complex origins related to power, sadism, and masochism which result in hazardous persons in the form of serial killers, rapists and other deviants?**

There are many components in the mind of a sexual deviant. It is more than just the individual. It is more than the individual's childhood environment. Always bear in mind that every individual existed before the appearance of its present material body. The individual had past lives, and carries packages of complex dysfunction from the past.

We cannot see that past but like in every other incidence we should be aware that there is some contribution from time past.

**What is happening to the individual psychically before, during and after masturbation? Is the energy which causes the individual to commit the act solely his or her energy or a combination of several influences?**

This is simple to answer: The individual is possessed by a composite person-energy which assumed the form of a compelling urge.

**Does masturbation have long term effects on the subtle body and if so can it be corrected or reversed?**

The long term effect is that of habit. Any habit compels the subtle body to act for fulfillments again and again, and without respect to the social, psychological or environmental cost. To reverse or correct a habit one has to reduce the instances of its memory and one should also cultivate another habit to absorb the psychological groove to be vacated by the undesirable one.

As soon as the memory of the old habit is effectively suppressed, the incidences of it will be reduced but there will be a blank space which should be filled with a new constructive habit.

**How would you explain the incidence of a man who had only a sexual attraction to a co-worker**

**but no physical sexual contact? He felt compelled to masturbate while having fantasies about intercourse with this person. He said that even though he is no longer employed at the same place, still these fantasies arise and compel him to masturbate.**

In such a situation an ancestor either from his background, or from the co-worker, feels that the union of these two is desirable. If such a union occurred and there was no contraceptive means and the two were sexually potent, we would find out who that ancestor was in about 9 months, when it would come out of the woman's body as an infant.

Obviously this man is possessed by an ancestor who is so strongly attracted to this couple and who wishes so much for the union of this couple, that the man feels a compulsion to masturbate, which yields up for the ancestor sexual emissions which if they were being deposited into the body of the co-worker would result in a pregnancy and then that specific urge would stop in him because of the ancestor being involved in the formation of its fetus.

# Index

# Author

Michael Beloved (Yogi *Madhvacarya)* teaches kundalini yoga and inSelf Yoga© meditation. He carefully studied the sexual behavior of human bodies, particularly his own, to tap into the origins of the sexual urge. His yoga practice made it compelling to study the kundalini life force which is the exploiter of sexual pleasures in animal forms, human or otherwise.

Recently some students of kundalini yoga inquired about the event of masturbation, as to its necessity and elimination. To explain that and to give psychic insight, this book was composed.

# Series

## Commentaries

**Yoga Sutras of Patanjali**

**Meditation Expertise**

**Krishna Cosmic Body**

**Bhagavad Gita Explained**

**Anu Gita Explained**

**Kriya Yoga Bhagavad Gita**

**Brahma Yoga Bhagavad Gita**

**Uddhava Gita Explained**

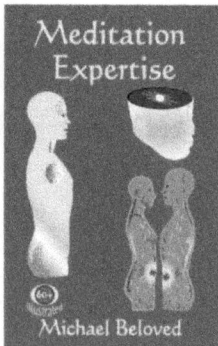

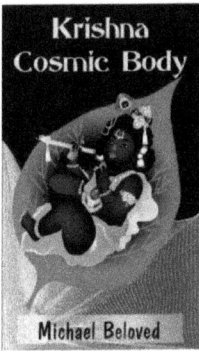

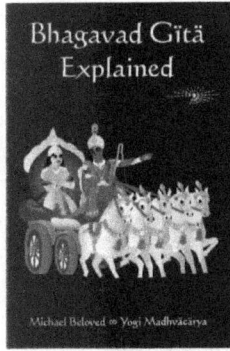

**Yoga Sutras of Patanjali** is the globally acclaimed text book of yoga. This has detailed expositions of yoga techniques. Many kriya techniques are vividly described in the commentary.

**Meditation Expertise** is an analysis and application of the Yoga Sutras. This book is loaded with illustrations and has detailed explanations of secretive advanced meditation techniques which are called kriyas in the Sanskrit language.

**Krishna Cosmic Body** is a narrative commentary on the Markandeya Samasya portion of the Aranyaka Parva of the Mahabharata. This is the detailed description of the dissolution of the world, as experienced by the great yogin Markandeya who transcended the cosmic deity, Brahma, and reached Brahma's source who is a divine infant Krishna.

**Bhagavad Gita Explained** shows what was said in the Gita without religious overtones and sectarian biases.

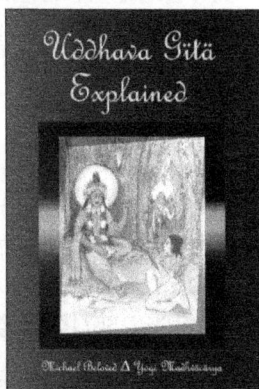

**Anu Gita Explained** is the detailed description of the effect-energy of current actions in application to future lives.

**Kriya Yoga Bhagavad Gita** shows the instructions for those who are doing kriya yoga.

**Brahma Yoga Bhagavad Gita** shows the instructions for those who are doing brahma yoga.

**Uddhava Gita Explained** shows the instructions to Uddhava which are more advanced than the ones given to Arjuna.

Bhagavad Gita is an instruction for applying the expertise of yoga in the cultural field. This is why the process taught to Arjuna is called karma yoga which means karma + yoga or cultural activities done with a yogic demeanor.

Uddhava Gita is an instruction for apply the expertise of yoga to attaining spiritual status. This is why it is explains jnana yoga and bhakti yoga in detail. Jnana yoga is using mystic skill for knowing the spiritual part of existence. Bhakti yoga is for developing affectionate relationships with divine beings.

Karma yoga is for negotiating the social concerns in the material world and therefore it is inferior to bhakti yoga which concerns negotiating the social concerns in the spiritual world.

This world has a social environment and the spiritual world has one too.

Right now Uddhava Gita is the most advanced informative spiritual book on the planet. There is nothing anywhere which is superior to it or which goes into so much detail as it. It verified that historically Krishna is the most advanced human being to ever have left literary instructions on this planet. Even Patanjali Yoga Sutras which I translated and gave an application for in my book, **Meditation Expertise**, does not go as far as the Uddhava Gita.

Some of the information of these two books is identical but while the Yoga Sutras are concerned with the personal spiritual emancipation (kaivalyam) of the individual spirits, the Uddhava Gita explains that and also explains the situations in the spiritual universes.

Bhagavad Gita is from the *Mahabharata* which is the history of the Pandavas. Arjuna, the student of the Gita, is one of the Pandavas brothers. He was in a social hassle and did not know how to apply yoga expertise to solve it. Krishna gave him a crash-course on the battlefield about that.

Uddhava Gita is from the *Srimad Bhagavatam (Bhagavata Purana),* which is a history of the incarnations of Krishna. Uddhava was a relative of Krishna. He was concerned about the situation of the deaths of many of his relatives but Krishna diverted Uddhava's attention to the practice of yoga for the purpose of successfully migrating to the spiritual environment.

# Explained Series

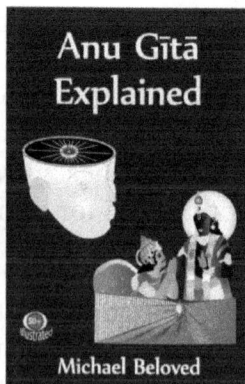

**Bhagavad Gita Explained**

**Anu Gita Explained**

**Uddhava Gita Explained**

The specialty of these books is that they are free of missionary intentions, cult tactics and philosophical distortion. Instead of using these books to add credence to a philosophy, meditation process, belief or plea for followers, I spread the information out so that a reader can look through this literature and freely take or leave anything as desired.

When Krishna stressed himself as God, I stated that. When Krishna laid no claims for supremacy, I showed that. The reader is left to form an independent opinion about the validity of the information and the credibility of Krishna.

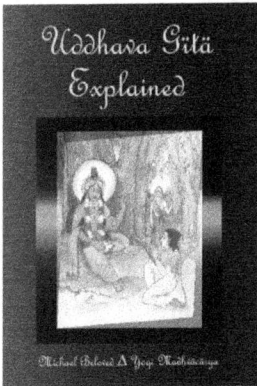

There is a difference in the discourse with Arjuna in the Bhagavad Gita and the one with Uddhava in the Uddhava Gita. In fact these two books may appear to contradict each other. In the Bhagavad Gita, Krishna pressured Arjuna to complete social duties. In the Uddhava Gita, Krishna insisted that Uddhava should abandon the same.

The Anu Gita is completely different to the Bhagavad Gita. Krishna refused to display the Universal Form. He quoted a siddha from a higher dimension who lectured on the effect-energies of actions as these construct a person's future opportunities.

# Meditation Series

## Meditation Pictorial

## Meditation Expertise

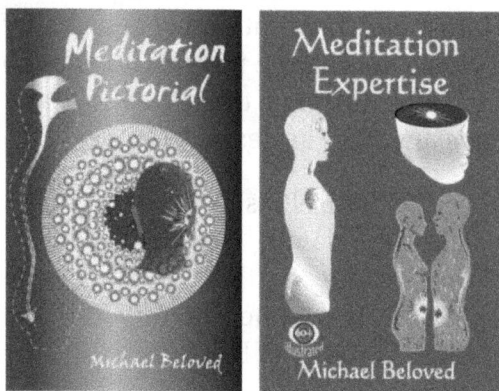

The specialty of these books is the mind diagrams which profusely illustrate what is written. This shows exactly what one has to do mentally to develop and then sustain a meditation practice.

In the **Meditation Pictorial**, one is shown how to develop psychic insight, a feature without which meditation is imagination and visualization, without any mystic experience per se.

In the **Meditation Expertise**, one is shown how to coral one's practice to bring it in line with the classic syllabus of yoga which Patanjali lays out as the ashtanga yoga 8-staged practice.

Both books are profusely illustrated with mind diagrams showing the components of psychic consciousness and the inner design of the subtle body.

## Specialty Topics

### sex you!

The mystery of sex and reincarnation is explained in detail, not in terms of religion or superstition but by psychic facts which any individual can observe, if he or she can shift focus to the psychic plane. Books like the Bardo Thodol (Tibetan Book of the Dead) and the Egyptian Book of the Dead (Papyrus of Ani), along with Bhagavad Gita, the reincarnation teaching of Buddha and other vital books, took humanity through a spiritual technological leap through time into the hereafter. Perhaps none of these texts dealt with the incidences of sex and reincarnation head on, especially the link between you and the sexual act of your parents which produced your body. In this book you get the details in plain terms without mystery and religious impositions.

## Spiritual Master

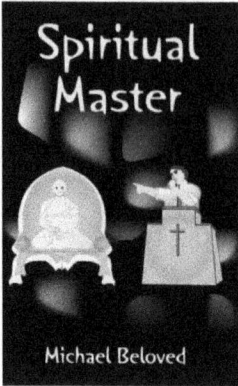

Practically every positive and negative aspect of having a guru is discussed in this book with recommendations of how to deal with gurus safely. A non-proficient guru can be useful despite his faults, but one must know how to side-step hassles and get to the business at hand, which is to get effective techniques from a spiritual master.

In some cases the spiritual master will be a complete fraud but one should not let that deter one from making spiritual progress in his association. "But why," one might ask, "should one stay with a fraudulent guru?" The answer is that if providence puts one in that position, one should honor providence but one should do so without getting hurt by the unqualified spiritual master. This and similar topics are discussed in this book.

## Sleep Paralysis

--- A short to-the-point paper on the psychic cause of sleep paralysis, how to manage it and decrease incidences.

The relationship between sleep paralysis and astral projection is explained. The methods of decreasing the incidences of sleep paralysis, increasing dream recall and being objectively conscious during astral projections is described.

The most revealing part of this paper is the author's description of his sleep paralysis states and what he did to contain these, get out of these and cause his psychic self to separate from and to fuse into the physical body without an incidence.

## Astral Projection

--- A paper on reincarnation, subtle body, astral projection, lucid dreaming, sleep paralysis, dimensional hoping, translation to paradise and transit to supernatural places. Astral Projection is a natural psychic function which is not reliant on the conscious awareness of the person concerned. Day after day usually once within every twenty-four hours, an individual spirit is displaced from its physical body but this is usually done while it is in a condition of stupor, where it is not aware that it was separated. It then becomes conscious again as a physical body and gets busy to restart its activities. Astral projection is really the observation of that displaced psyche. Information of how to become conscious of this is divulged in this paper.

# English Series

**Bhagavad Gita English**

**Anu Gita English**

**Markandeya Samasya English**

**Yoga Sutras English**

**Uddhava Gita English**

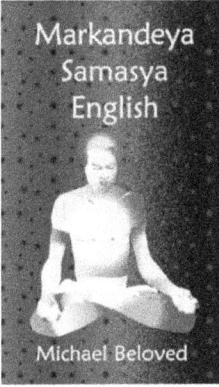

Markandeya Samasya English — Michael Beloved

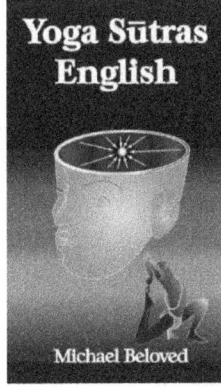

Yoga Sūtras English — Michael Beloved

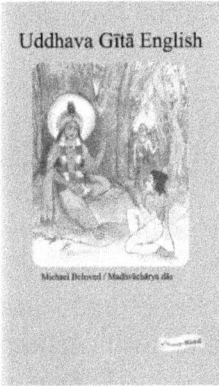

Uddhava Gītā English — Michael Beloved / Madhvāchārya das

These are in 21st Century English, very precise and exacting. Many Sanskrit words which were considered untranslatable into a Western language are rendered in precise, expressive and modern English, due to the English language becoming the world's universal means of concept conveyance.

Three of these books are instructions from Krishna. **In Bhagavad Gita English** and **Anu Gita English**, the instructions were for Arjuna. In the **Uddhava Gita English,** it was for Uddhava. Bhagavad Gita and Anu Gita are extracted from the Mahabharata. Uddhava Gita was extracted from the 11th Canto of the Srimad Bhagavatam (Bhagavata Purana). One of these books, the **Markandeya Samasya English** is about Krishna, as described by Yogi Markandeya, who survived the cosmic collapse and reached a divine child in whose transcendental body, the collapsed world was existing. Another of these books, the **Yoga Sutras English,** is the detailed syllabus about yoga practice.

My suggestion is that you read Bhagavad Gita English, the Anu Gita English, the Markandeya Samasya English, the Yoga Sutras English and lastly the Uddhava Gita English, which is much more complicated and detailed.

For each of these books we have at least one commentary, which is published separately. Thus your particular interest can be researched further in the commentaries.

The smallest of these commentaries and perhaps the simplest is the one for the Anu Gita. We published its commentary as the <u>Anu Gita Explained</u>. The Bhagavad Gita explanations were published in three distinct targeted commentaries. The first is <u>Bhagavad Gita Explained</u>, which sheds lights on how people in the time of Krishna and Arjuna regarded the information and applied it. Bhagavad Gita is an exposition of the application of yoga practice to cultural activities, which is known in the Sanskrit language as karma yoga.

Interestingly, Bhagavad Gita was spoken on a battlefield just before one of the greatest battles in the ancient world. A warrior, Arjuna, lost his wits and had no idea that he could apply his training in yoga to political dealings. Krishna, his charioteer, lectured on the spur of the moment to give Arjuna the skill of using yoga proficiency in cultural dealings including how to deal with corrupt officials on a battlefield.

The second commentary is the <u>Kriya Yoga Bhagavad Gita</u>. This clears the air about Krishna's information on the science of kriya yoga, showing that its techniques are clearly described free of charge to anyone who takes the time to read Bhagavad Gita. Kriya yoga concerns the battlefield which is the psyche of the living being. The internal war and the mental and emotional forces which are hostile to self-realization are dealt with in the kriya yoga practice.

The third commentary is the <u>Brahma Yoga Bhagavad Gita</u>. This shows what Krishna had to say outright and what he hinted about which concerns the brahma yoga practice, a mystic process for those who mastered kriya yoga.

There is one commentary for the **Markandeya Samasya English**. The title of that publication is <u>Krishna Cosmic Body</u>.

There are two commentaries to the Yoga Sutras. One is the <u>Yoga Sutras of Patanjali</u> and the other is the <u>Meditation Expertise</u>. These give detailed explanations of the process of Yoga.

For the Uddhava Gita, we published the <u>Uddhava Gita Explained</u>. This is a large book and requires concentration and study for integration of the information. Of the books which deal with transcendental topics, my opinion is that the discourse between Krishna and Uddhava has the complete information about the realities in existence. This book is the one which removes massive existential ignorance.

## Website:

**michaelbeloved.com**

## Forum:

**inselfyoga.com**

## Contact:

**axisnexus@gmail.com**